THE TIANANMEN SQUARE MASSACRE

BY WIL MARA

CHILDREN'S PRESS®

An Imprint of Scholastic Inc.
New York Toronto London Auckland Sydney
Mexico City New Delhi Hong Kong
Danbury, Connecticut

BRINGING HISTORY to LIFE

Content Consultant
James Marten, PhD
Professor and Chair, History Department
Marquette University
Milwaukee, Wisconsin

Library of Congress Cataloging-in-Publication Data
Mara, Wil.
 The Tiananmen Square massacre / by Wil Mara.
  pages cm.—(Cornerstones of freedom)
 Includes bibliographical references and index.
 ISBN 978-0-531-28207-6 (lib. bdg.) — ISBN 978-0-531-27672-3 (pbk.)
 1. China—History—Tiananmen Square Incident, 1989—Juvenile literature.
 I. Title.
 DS779.32.M34 2013
 951.05'8—dc23   2013000081

All rights reserved. Published in 2014 by Children's Press, an imprint of
Scholastic Inc.
Printed in the United States of America 113

SCHOLASTIC, CHILDREN'S PRESS, CORNERSTONES OF FREEDOM™,
and associated logos are trademarks and/or registered trademarks of
Scholastic Inc.

1 2 3 4 5 6 7 8 9 10 R 23 22 21 20 19 18 17 16 15 14

Photographs © 2014: Alamy Images: 6 (Imagestate Media Partners
Limited - Impact Photos), 7 (MARKA); AP Images: 35, 57 bottom (Boris
Yurchenko), back cover, 46 (Jeff Widener), 37, 57 top (Kyodo News), 16,
27 (Mark Avery), 5 top, 54 (Pablo Martinez Monsivais), 4 top, 29 (Sadayuki
Mikami), 40 (Tsugufumi Matsumoto), 32 (Xinhua), 8, 24, 34, 56; Corbis
Images: 12 (Alain Nogues/Sygma), 5 bottom, 20 (Baldev), 14 (Bohemian
Nomad Picturemakers), 10 (Dean Conger), 28, 44 (Durand-Langevin/
Sygma), 43 (Jacques Langevin/Sygma), 22 (Patrick Durand/Sygma), 2,
3, 13, 25, 36 (Peter Turnley); Getty Images: 33 (Catherine Henriette/AFP),
26 (Chris Niedenthal/Time Life Pictures), 38 (Cynthia Johnson/Time Life
Pictures), 49 (Frederic J. Brown/AFP), 11 (Marie Mathelin/Roger Viollet),
50 (Mark Ralston/AFP), 4 bottom, 15 (Nelson Ching/Bloomberg), 45 (Peter
Charlesworth/LightRocket), cover (Robyn Beck/AFP), 17 (Sandro Tucci/
Time Life Pictures); Shutterstock, Inc./TonyV3112: 55; The Image Works:
51 (Fritz Hoffmann), 18 (Lee Snider), 42 (Sean Ramsay), 30 (Steve Lehman/
Impact/HIP), 19 (Xinhua/ullstein bild).

Maps by XNR Productions, Inc.

Did you know that studying history can be fun?

BRING HISTORY TO LIFE by becoming a history investigator. Examine the evidence (primary and secondary source materials); cross-examine the people and witnesses. Take a look at what was happening at the time—but be careful! What happened years ago might suddenly become incredibly interesting and change the way you think!

Contents

A Long Time Coming

Many of the Chinese protesters hoping to make China more democratic during the Tiananmen Square incident were students and other young people.

The horrifying events that unfolded in Tiananmen Square in early June 1989 were among the most significant to occur in China during the 20th century. They were brought about by the clash between two groups with

TIANANMEN SQUARE WAS

opposing political views. One group was made up of people who wanted to move China closer to **democracy**. They were mostly young people as well as those in the working class. The other group was made up of people who did not want such changes. They were mostly middle-age and older men who were high-ranking members of the **Communist** Party of China (CPC).

The CPC took full control of the country in late 1949. Its leader was a man named Mao Zedong. Mao was highly intelligent and a skilled politician. He eventually began implementing his personal political philosophy—a collection of social and political beliefs based on communism that is known as Maoism.

Mao Zedong led the Communist Party of China until his death in 1976.

CONSTRUCTED IN 1651.

CHAPTER 1

THE WINDS OF CHANGE

Deng Xiaoping (left) became involved with communism while studying in France and the Soviet Union during the 1920s.

BY THE TIME MAO DIED IN 1976, many Chinese citizens had grown frustrated with Maoism. They wanted more personal freedoms as well as more professional success. They also began calling for a more open and transparent form of government. Mao's successor, Deng Xiaoping, had supported communism all his life. But he also acknowledged the growing unrest and dissatisfaction among the Chinese people. He felt that the time had come to modify Maoism and usher in a new age of Chinese government. Deng believed that one of the keys to a healthy and more productive future for China was **reform** to its **economy**. He wanted to begin introducing small elements of **capitalism** into it.

Rice is one of the most widely grown crops in China.

Stage One

With the help of his supporters in the CPC, Deng began
the first stage of his reforms in December 1978. One feature
allowed farmers not only to own their farmlands, but also
to keep and sell what they grew after giving a set percentage
to the government. This gave farmers the incentive to
be much more productive, which earned them greater
profits. It also reduced the risk of national food shortages.
For many farming families, this led to a better quality of
life than they had ever known. Another feature of Deng's
reforms was permission for ordinary citizens to own and
run small businesses. Scores of budding business owners
took advantage of these new opportunities. This resulted

in skyrocketing incomes for citizens who had previously worked in government-assigned jobs.

The first stage of Deng's plan also opened China to foreign **investment** for the first time since the early 20th century. This allowed people from other countries to put their money into growing Chinese businesses in which the government had minimal involvement. Investment money soon began pouring in.

During the 1980s, Chinese citizens, such as this shoe repairman in the city of Chongqing, were allowed to have their own small businesses.

In 1979, not long after assuming leadership of China, Deng Xiaoping delivered a speech outlining his goals for the future of the CPC. See page 60 for a link to read the English translation of part of the speech online.

In spite of these reforms, the Chinese government under Deng's leadership was still communist at heart. It still wielded tremendous power over its people. The CPC continued to control the largest industries, set price limitations, and intervene in all other areas of Chinese society whenever it wanted. Nevertheless, these early economic reforms were welcomed by millions as a step in the right direction.

In the early years of Deng's leadership, factories and other large businesses in China continued to be controlled almost entirely by the CPC.

As Deng loosened government control over large industries, China grew in importance as a worldwide center of manufacturing.

Stage Two

The second stage of Deng's reforms began in 1984. This period was characterized by a continuing decrease in the control the government had over businesses. The government mostly left smaller businesses in the hands of their owners, with some interaction by local or provincial governments. Some of the larger industries also had less government influence. They were run and even co-owned for the first time by private citizens.

China's wealthiest and best educated citizens were largely unaffected by rising inflation during the 1980s.

In spite of this period of growth and prosperity, all was not perfect. Industries that were still largely controlled by the CPC soon began losing money. There were also wild bursts of **inflation**. Because Deng's plan called for less government control over prices, the cost of some goods and services became so high that only the wealthiest citizens could afford them.

Most of the troubles that arose from the transition into a new economic system were expected by Deng and his supporters. They held steady in their belief that the economic reforms would be best for the nation in the long run. There were some in the CPC, however, who believed otherwise. The idea of increased economic opportunities for the general public made them uneasy. Such freedoms would mean less government control. As time went on, the CPC began to split into two distinct sides. Those who supported Deng's reforms and wanted to continue expanding them were called the reformers. Those who wanted to halt them or even reverse them were known as the hard-liners.

SPOTLIGHT ON

The Communist Party of China

The Communist Party of China, often referred to as the CPC, began in Shanghai in 1921. It got off to a rocky start, as China was going through great political and social upheaval following the end of its dynastic era. During this era, which lasted thousands of years, the nation was ruled by a series of powerful families. The end of this era left a new gap in China's power structure. As a result, several political factions were vying for control. The CPC's main rival was the Kuomintang, or National People's Party. While the CPC supported a communist approach to government, the Kuomintang wanted to be more democratic. This conflict led to the Chinese Civil War, which raged from 1927 to 1950. The CPC emerged victorious and is still the ruling government in mainland China. It has more than 75 million members today, making it the largest political party in the world.

Supportive but Frustrated

Before Deng's reforms, a Chinese citizen would receive a job, health care, and other benefits from the government. But under a **free market** economy, there were more incidents of layoffs, reduced work hours, and inadequate job training. Job opportunities for young men and women were often scarce.

Many young people in China were disappointed with the jobs available to them after they worked hard in school to develop useful skills.

In spite of this, most young people supported Deng's reforms, but they expected the CPC to help them find work. Once they did find jobs, they often encountered difficulty getting ahead in their careers. This was because many of the more powerful members of Chinese society—including governmental figures and the few who were very wealthy—received special treatment. For example, the son or daughter of a high-ranking CPC member might be given a job over other candidates who were more qualified. This outraged many young people.

YESTERDAY'S HEADLINES

Reaction to Deng Xiaoping's economic reforms varied widely in the U.S. media. Some journalists appeared to be skeptical that the reforms would work, while others were more open-minded. In the January 28, 1985, edition of the *New York Times*, journalist John Burns wrote a piece titled "After 4,000 Civilized Years, China Starts to Hurry." Burns praised Deng for realizing the value of a society that encouraged productivity in its citizens. "From Deng Xiaoping's hosting of foreign investors at the Great Hall of the People," he wrote, "to the new merchant class springing up in the street bazaars [above], the idea of time as precious is bandied about as though nobody ever thought of it before."

Even today, the Chinese government continues to maintain strong control over newspapers and other media.

Frustration grew in other areas of daily life as well. Many citizens wanted freedom of speech, freedom of the media, and improved working conditions. They even hoped for greater private control of business and full transparency from their government. These were advantages that many people around the rest of the world had long enjoyed. In the United States, for example, television stations and newspapers were allowed to run any stories they wanted. In China, however, the government controlled all such media.

Similarly, an ordinary citizen in the United States could openly criticize the government. In China, such bold opinions could lead to severe punishment.

By the late 1980s, millions of young and working-class Chinese had been given a taste of capitalism, and they wanted more. But many of the CPC hard-liners now felt very threatened. Most of them had only grudgingly gone along with Deng's reforms in the first place. Deng and his supporters found themselves at the center of a potentially explosive situation.

As Deng Xiaoping (right) worked to give the Chinese people what they wanted, the CPC hard-liners grew more uneasy with the reforms.

CHAPTER 2

BATTLE LINES ARE DRAWN

Student protests grew larger and larger as China's young people became more upset over their situation.

IN LATE 1985 AND EARLY 1986, crowds of ordinary citizens began taking to the streets to express their discontent. Most of these people were students. They were young and angry at their poor prospects within a new economy that was supposed to offer so much. They were supported by an increasingly angry working class.

Before helping to inspire the Tiananmen Square protests, Fang Lizhi was a world renowned astrophysicist who helped found the physics department of Beijing's University of Science and Technology of China.

Inspiring the Masses

These early protests were inspired in part by the speeches and writings of a Chinese professor named Fang Lizhi. Fang was an astrophysicist by education, but he was also an open-minded thinker who believed China needed to move farther away from Maoism and embrace a more democratic style of society. He had spent some time in the United States, where he was exposed to all the freedoms and privileges that the average American citizen enjoys every day. He was eager to share his observations back home. Fang was very popular among students and working-class citizens. He gave numerous lectures and wrote essays that were eagerly read by ordinary people. His standing with the CPC, however, was shaky at best. There were times when he was banned from the party for his opinions.

A Martyr Emerges

The government's hard-liners became greatly alarmed by the growing unrest among the citizens. Deng Xiaoping knew he could no longer sit back and just hope for the best. He asked one of his leading supporters and oldest friends, Hu Yaobang, to formally remove Fang and others from the CPC. This was more a gesture to please the hard-liners than anything else. But Hu refused to follow Deng's orders. As a result, Hu was forced to give up his position within the CPC in early January 1987. In turn, he became something of a folk hero to many Chinese citizens.

A FIRSTHAND LOOK AT
FANG LIZHI'S "DEMOCRACY, REFORM, AND MODERNIZATION"

In 1986, Fang Lizhi delivered a speech at Tongji University in Shanghai. His words inspired the millions of Chinese citizens who were irritated by their lack of progress within the CPC's communist system. Many in China consider his words as relevant today as they were back then. See page 60 for a link to read an English translation of the speech online.

Once Hu was gone, the hard-liners made great efforts to smear his reputation through the media. They strongly implied that he was an enemy of communism and a traitor. This effort went on for years and infuriated millions. Then, in mid-April 1989, Hu suffered a heart attack and died. Many close to him blamed the attack on the stress he endured as a result of the CPC's crusade to humiliate him.

SPOTLIGHT ON

Hu Yaobang

Hu Yaobang was involved in Chinese politics from a very early age. He took part in a rebellion when he was just 12 years old, formally joined the CPC at 14, and was a full member of the communist party by his early twenties. He was a strong supporter of Mao Zedong and Maoism early on, but his views changed over time. He first met Deng Xiaoping in the 1930s and fought alongside him during the Chinese Civil War. By the 1980s, Deng considered Hu one of his most-trusted friends and helped him advance quickly through the ranks of the CPC. Hu became second only to Deng. He dedicated himself to implementing Deng's reformist policies, which earned him numerous enemies among the party's hard-liners.

The Pot Begins to Boil

In reaction to Hu's death, crowds began to assemble to mourn and celebrate his legacy. At first, the crowds were made

Protesters gathered in Tiananmen Square and other locations throughout China to pay tribute to Hu Yaobang after his death in April 1989.

up mostly of students, but they soon began to include many other groups of people. These gatherings occurred on university grounds and in public places, mostly in Beijing. One of the largest groups of mourners came together at a large public plaza known as Tiananmen Square. By the night of April 17, just two days after Hu's death, thousands had gathered there.

At first, the student **demonstrations** were peaceful. However, they became increasingly hostile as the demonstrators accused the government of being too

Journalists and photographers from around the world traveled to Beijing to document the protests in Tiananmen Square.

self-serving and insensitive. The official obituary that the CPC issued for Hu, for example, praised him as a noble warrior and a statesman. Hu's admirers believed the hard-liners wrote such positive remarks just to cover up their mistreatment of him.

Outraged, the demonstrators sent a list of demands to the government on April 20. The demands included the end of state-controlled media, greater transparency among government officials, and public admission that removing Hu from power in 1987 was wrong.

The Government Miscalculates

The Chinese government had no intention of giving in to the demonstrators' demands. It did, however, try to please them by giving Hu a formal state funeral on April 22. It was held at the Great Hall of the People, located in the western section of Tiananmen Square. However, this backfired. The funeral was attended by several government officials responsible for Hu's downfall, and the eulogy was very brief.

Rather than pacifying the demonstrators, the official state funeral for Hu Yaobang only served to inspire more protests.

北京理工大学

北京理工大学

YESTERDAY'S HEADLINES

Hu Yaobang was given a surprising amount of respect around the world. Among the many foreign reporters who covered China (above), one American wrote, "In a nation where caution is often prized, [Hu] was the exception. … When he was asked which of Mao's thoughts were applicable in China's efforts to modernize its economy, he is reported to have replied, 'I think, none.'"

Daniel Southerland, writing for the *Washington Post*, sensed the reaction that would come from Hu's passing. "The death of Hu could provide a spark for more wall-poster protests and possibly demonstrations by students, who have been under pressure not to march in the streets for democracy." Given the events of the days and weeks that followed, Southerland's comments were remarkably insightful.

The government had ordered Tiananmen Square closed for the funeral, but about 100,000 students staged a demonstration there during the service. They asked to meet with Li Peng, one of the highest-ranking hard-liners of the CPC at the time. This request was denied.

Four days later, on April 26, the government issued an **editorial** in one of the nation's leading newspapers. It claimed that the demonstrators' goal was to overthrow the CPC, and it warned that future protests would be handled with unforgiving force. Instead of making the

Police struggled to control the thousands of protesters heading toward Tiananmen Square on April 27, 1989.

demonstrators more fearful, it had the opposite effect. It not only enraged them, but also created more sympathy for them among millions of other citizens. The day after the article ran, about 50,000 students in the Beijing area organized another march on Tiananmen Square. This time, thousands of ordinary Chinese citizens openly showed their support. The CPC, more nervous than ever, became convinced that the situation was growing out of control—and that more serious action had to be taken.

CHAPTER 3

MARTIAL LAW

Government officials met with protesters in an effort to end the conflict peacefully.

HOPING TO SQUELCH THE mounting tension, the CPC sent representatives to speak with the protesting students. Major issues were finally discussed, but no promises of meaningful change came from the government. Just as members of the government were split between the hard-liners and the reformers, there were now two similar groups emerging among the demonstrators. Some still trusted the government and were willing to work with them. Others were increasingly suspicious and unwilling to give in.

Zhao Ziyang (holding megaphone, facing forward) served as general secretary of the CPC from 1987 until 1989.

A World Spectacle

General secretary Zhao Ziyang was one of the highest-ranking members of the CPC and a dedicated reformer. He got involved with the struggle between protesters and the CPC in early May. Zhao gave speeches to tell the demonstrators that he understood their anger and supported the changes they wanted. He said he would bring their concerns back to the government. As a result of Zhao's efforts, many demonstrators felt they had a new ally in a powerful position. They hoped that Zhao could be a replacement for Hu Yaobang. Most of the demonstrations soon came to an end, and a potential crisis seemed to have been averted. This was not the case, however.

A FIRSTHAND LOOK AT
THE APRIL 26 EDITORIAL

The CPC's April 26 editorial eventually went down in history as one of the most ill-considered media maneuvers ever made by the party. The government had hoped to scare the demonstrators into obedience. Instead, it helped cause exactly the "chaotic state" it aimed to avoid. See page 60 for a link to read an English translation of the editorial online.

When Zhao went back to the CPC to discuss the demonstrators' demands, he was met with strong opposition. At the same time, some of the students insisted on more direct conversations with government representatives. They felt Zhao had tricked them into backing down, and they became more determined

Protesters who trusted Zhao became angry when he was unable to fulfill his promises to them.

than ever. On May 13, the demonstrators attempted to gain some worldwide attention by staging a **hunger strike**. More than a quarter million protesters were in Tiananmen. Millions more around the country openly expressed their support. Some held smaller demonstrations of their own.

The Tiananmen demonstrators thought their timing was particularly effective because the CPC was expecting a visit from Mikhail Gorbachev, the leader of the Soviet Union, two days later. It was to be the first meeting between Soviet and Chinese leaders in years, and Gorbachev's welcoming ceremony was to take place in Tiananmen Square. The students believed that the CPC would not want to risk being embarrassed in front of the Soviet leader.

Some demonstrators drew attention to their cause by refusing to eat until their demands were met.

The Chinese government was concerned that the protests in Beijing would affect Deng Xiaoping's meeting with Soviet leader Mikhail Gorbachev (right) at the Great Hall of the People in Beijing.

Deng Xiaoping asked Zhao Ziyang to find a way to remove the demonstrators before Gorbachev's visit. Zhao understood the need to do this, but he still did not want to use force. He went to Tiananmen in person and tried to make the demonstrators understand the importance of the meeting. But the students refused to leave. They repeated their original demands and also insisted that the CPC formally apologize for the April 26 editorial. Instead of agreeing to these demands, the government moved the welcoming ceremony to the airport where Gorbachev landed. This angered many influential

By early May, the crowd of protesters in Tiananmen Square had grown to more than a quarter of a million people.

members of the CPC. Some who were previously undecided about their feelings toward the demonstrators now sided with the hard-liners.

At the same time, the demonstrators were rapidly gaining support elsewhere. The news that their hunger strike had managed to alter official government plans spread around the world. In Beijing alone, more than a million citizens began to take part in demonstrations in Tiananmen Square and elsewhere around the city. The demonstrators were no longer just students. They were people of all ages, professions, and backgrounds. Smaller demonstrations also flared up in more than 400 other Chinese towns and cities.

The CPC Regains the Upper Hand

Reformist members of the CPC, such as Zhao, now found themselves in a difficult position—the demonstrators had embarrassed the government during the Gorbachev visit while the rest of the world watched. The CPC's hard-liners urged Deng Xiaoping to deal with the demonstrators with force. They wanted to declare a state of martial law. Under martial law, the government could use its military to regain order. Deng felt he had little choice in the matter, and martial law was soon approved.

At the same time, support for the Tiananmen demonstrators continued to grow. More than 250,000

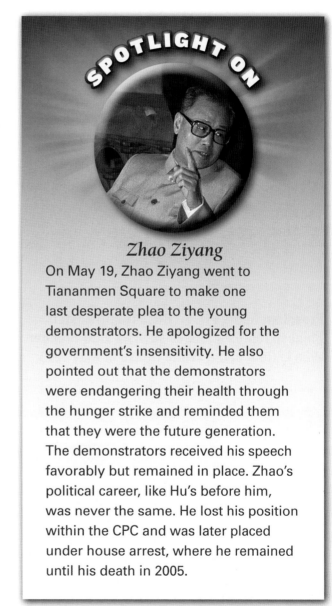

SPOTLIGHT ON

Zhao Ziyang

On May 19, Zhao Ziyang went to Tiananmen Square to make one last desperate plea to the young demonstrators. He apologized for the government's insensitivity. He also pointed out that the demonstrators were endangering their health through the hunger strike and reminded them that they were the future generation. The demonstrators received his speech favorably but remained in place. Zhao's political career, like Hu's before him, was never the same. He lost his position within the CPC and was later placed under house arrest, where he remained until his death in 2005.

people came together in Hong Kong, and a parade the following day drew a crowd of more than 1.5 million. New demonstrations began in towns and cities around the world where there were large populations of Chinese citizens.

Regardless, the CPC continued to refuse the demonstrators' requests for high-level discussions. They also disregarded pleas from other leaders around the world. U.S. president George H. W. Bush, for example, met with a CPC representative around this time and urged the party to be understanding of the demonstrators. Back in China, however, the leadership decided that the time had come to end the demonstrations once and for all.

Standoff

On May 20, military vehicles loaded with armed soldiers left various bases in the Beijing area and began

President George H. W. Bush (right) hosted Chinese representatives such as Vice Premier Wan Li (left) at the White House in May 1989.

heading toward the square. On the way, they were blocked by thousands of supporters of the Tiananmen demonstrators. The soldiers were not attacked, but rather treated as if they were victims of a cruel and controlling leadership. They were given food and water and asked to join in the protests. The soldiers were delayed for four days until the government finally ordered them to return to their bases.

This was seen by some people as another victory for the demonstrators. Many believed it was a sign that the government was finally ready to give in to their demands. In truth, the increasingly nervous government saw it as proof that greater force was required to defeat the protesters.

A VIEW FROM ABROAD

Many of the world's nations followed developments of the Tiananmen situation through daily news reports. The Indian government, however, made the decision to minimize media coverage to their citizens because India was trying to build a better relationship with China at the time. This did not necessarily signal India's approval of the CPC's heavy-handed approach, but it did demonstrate the delicate nature of international diplomacy. A few foreign governments were openly supportive of the CPC's actions. Among them were North Korea, Cuba, and East Germany—all of which were communist at the time.

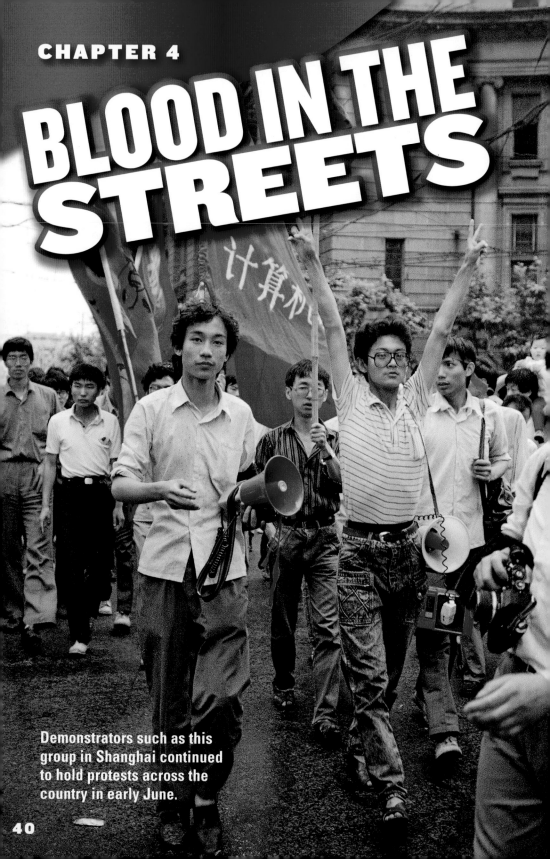

CHAPTER 4

BLOOD IN THE STREETS

Demonstrators such as this group in Shanghai continued to hold protests across the country in early June.

BY JUNE 1, THE CPC HARD-liners had reached their breaking point. They were eager to see the demonstrations brought to an end. Articles further criticizing the demonstrators began to appear in government-controlled newspapers. The articles emphasized that the demonstrators were somewhat disorganized, that they had no clear leader and no clear message, and that there was a fair amount of infighting in their ranks. This was true to a degree. The demonstrators had their own extreme and moderate factions, just as the Chinese government did. This led to occasional disagreements and some confusion as to who was in charge. However, the demonstrators were still united in their ultimate objectives. The newspaper articles only served to further anger them and make them more determined than ever in their fight for their cause.

Protesters in the Beijing streets constructed barriers and used their own bodies to block soldiers from reaching Tiananmen Square.

The Violence Begins

On June 2, the CPC ordered the military to mobilize once again, this time in even greater numbers. Troops began moving later that evening. Commanders had been told to end the demonstrations as peacefully as possible, but that they could use force if necessary. The troops approached from all directions. They planned to surround the square and then clear the demonstrators out of it. But in the streets leading to the square were tens of thousands of people who supported the demonstrators. They began setting up barriers again, using everything from vehicles to fences. When they ran out of things for building barriers, they simply stood in the military's way.

Shortly after 10:00 p.m. on June 3, with tension running higher and higher, the first round of bloodshed began. In the Muxidi section of Beijing, a short distance from Tiananmen Square, soldiers opened fire on the citizens blocking their path. In a matter of minutes, hundreds of people were either injured or dead. The soldiers' bullets also struck several people who were nearby, watching from their homes or apartments, but were not actually participating. To this day, it is unclear if the soldiers fired because they were attacked first or if they were simply following orders. There were some reports that the Tiananmen supporters had hurled rocks and flaming bottles of alcohol at them, and that some soldiers were grabbed by mobs and beaten.

Faced with the threat of violence from the Chinese military, demonstrators held their ground on June 3, 1989.

A FIRSTHAND LOOK AT
EYEWITNESS REPORTS

A few foreign journalists who were already in Beijing to cover Gorbachev's visit witnessed the carnage at Tiananmen Square firsthand. One reporter from England's BBC wrote, "Even though violence was expected, the ferocity of the attack took many by surprise." See page 60 for a link to read the full report online.

Some protesters fled the scene to escape the violence. Others chose to stand their ground, and a few even attempted to fight back as tempers raged on both sides. Many protesters who stayed were either shot, beaten, or arrested. A few who attempted to get away were chased down. Some military vehicles were set ablaze

Protesters used whatever vehicles they could find to remove the wounded from harm's way after the Chinese military opened fire on them.

Protesters tipped over large vehicles as fires raged and gunshots filled the air during the struggle against the military on June 4.

and destroyed. As word spread that the military was using live ammunition, some of the demonstrators in Tiananmen Square fled in fear for their lives.

The military reached Tiananmen Square shortly after midnight on June 4. The soldiers surrounded the square and awaited further instructions. Exactly what happened next has never been fully established. There are many conflicting accounts. It is widely believed that more chaos erupted as some demonstrators decided to stand their ground. It is possible that a few of them attempted to attack military personnel with more flaming alcohol bottles, rocks, sticks, and other weapons.

At around 4:00 a.m., protest leaders voted on whether they should leave the square or continue resisting. Though some wanted to stay, the vote ended up in favor of leaving. The protesters slowly began walking away as the military looked on.

By sunrise, the government had mostly succeeded in clearing out the square, and it regained control of the surrounding community a few days later. Demonstrations continued elsewhere in the country and around the world as word of the violence spread. Millions spoke out against the brutality of the Chinese government. Many people wore black armbands as a sign of solidarity with the Tiananmen demonstrators and as a symbol of grief for those who had been killed. Police and military forces squashed some of these demonstrations in the same way they had put them down in the streets of Beijing.

By June 5, tanks and soldiers were all that remained in Tiananmen Square.

Body Count

Precise figures on the number of dead and injured at Tiananmen Square remain uncertain. Depending on the source, the numbers range from several hundred to several thousand, including soldiers and local police. The most realistic estimate is likely somewhere between 200 and 500 dead, and about 5,000 to 7,000 wounded. However, countless people were denied medical treatment by official orders and may have died as a result of their injuries later on. It is also likely that the government eventually tracked down and imprisoned or killed key figures who took part in the demonstrations. In addition, there were people protesting in other parts of China

A VIEW FROM ABROAD

Most of the leading nations around the world were outraged by the CPC's handling of the Tiananmen crisis. Individually, many governments condemned the CPC through both words and actions. In the United States, president George H. W. Bush stopped all sales of military materials to China. The European Union did the same and also ended all financial assistance to the country. The Australian government gave all visiting Chinese students the right to remain in Australia for up to four years if they feared punishment upon returning home. Japan publicly condemned the Tiananmen killings and stopped all loans to China for several months.

who were killed or injured, but those numbers are rarely included in the count.

Witch Hunt

Immediately after the massacre, the CPC decided to remove party members who had been sympathetic to the demonstrators. To achieve this, the hard-liners employed tens of thousands of agents to investigate more than one million government employees. These agents examined both the professional and personal lives of every individual they deemed suspicious.

Government workers were not the only ones to suffer the CPC's wrath in the wake of Tiananmen Square. People who took part in the demonstrations, as well as many of their supporters, were also targeted. The CPC created a "most wanted" list bearing the names of those it had identified as leaders of the demonstrations. People were hauled into courts for brief trials and then executed. Others were sent to labor camps, where they were worked to exhaustion. Some managed to escape and find refuge in other nations. This often meant never seeing their relatives or stepping foot in their homeland again.

When this witch hunt was over, tens of thousands of people were arrested and imprisoned. They were taken from their homes or offices, often in broad daylight and in front of their families. Many were kept in horrible conditions, with no access to decent food, clean water, or a telephone. Some were tortured, and others were killed. The fate of many of these people is still unknown.

Like many Chinese officials, Bao Tong was forced out of power and jailed for several years following the Tiananmen Square massacre.

The Thought Police

Following the massacre, the CPC immediately reversed most of the media freedoms the Chinese people had been permitted during the reform years. Millions of books, movies, newspapers, and music albums were banned. Countless newspapers and publishing houses went out of business for being too dangerous to the CPC, and thousands of people lost their jobs.

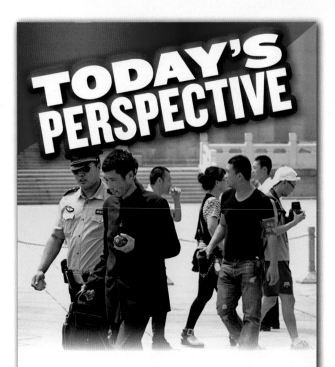

TODAY'S PERSPECTIVE

In June 2012, Robert Saiget of the Associated Free Press reported that Chinese authorities arrested (as shown above) countless people to prevent them from publicly observing the 23rd anniversary of the massacre. "Around 20 rights defenders were stopped by police and beaten this morning," one demonstrator told him. "The police said they were going to 'beat them to death.' They took about eight people into custody, including my husband. I fear he has been beaten badly." Saiget commented that, "Beijing still considers the incident a 'counter-revolutionary rebellion' and a 'political storm' and has refused to acknowledge any wrongdoing or consider compensation for those killed."

The CPC also slowed the pace of the economic reforms of previous years. This seemed unwise, because those changes were benefiting China as a whole. Realizing this, Deng Xiaoping continued to push for more free market improvements, and they did resume in the mid- to late 1990s. Officials even tried to shape the thinking about the massacre's effect on the country's progress. In 1999, a member of the CPC went so far as to say the way the government handled the Tiananmen situation was actually beneficial to China's economic

Small business began to thrive in China once again during the 1990s.

development. "If the way we handled the Tiananmen crisis was incorrect, we would not have today's prosperity," he said. "China would be in chaos. The people would have risen and resisted the government."

What Happened Where?

Beijing

As China's capital city, Beijing was the site of the largest protests during the events surrounding the Tiananmen Square massacre.

→ **Beijing** ⊛

CHINA

Shanghai ●

Shanghai

One of China's largest cities and an important trading center, Shanghai was the birthplace of the CPC. Like many other Chinese cities, it was the site of major protests around the time of the Tiananmen Square massacre.

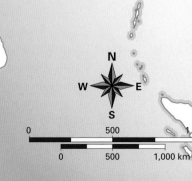

N
W ✦ E
S

0	500	1,000 mi
0	500	1,000 km

Muxidi

Shortly after 10:00 p.m. on June 3, the first bloodshed of the Tiananmen Square massacre occurred in the Muxidi section of Beijing as soldiers fired on citizens blocking their path, killing or injuring hundreds.

Great Hall of the People

Located on the western side of Tiananmen Square, the Great Hall of the People was the site of many important government events. Hu Yaobang's official state funeral was held there, and Soviet leader Mikhail Gorbachev and Deng Xiaoping met there during Gorbachev's 1989 visit.

Tiananmen Square

Tiananmen Square became the center of the Spring 1989 protests in China, drawing hundreds of thousands of demonstrators. On June 3, the Chinese government staged a violent intervention to force the protesters out of the square.

BEIJING

0   0.5   1 mi

0   0.5   1 km

Imperial Palace (Forbidden City)

Tiananmen Square

Muxidi

Great Hall of the People

What's Next?

The relationship between the United States and China has improved since the Tiananmen Square massacre. Here, President Obama meets with China's president Hu Jintao.

China's economy has continued to move closer to capitalism in the last few decades, much as Deng Xiaoping, Hu Yaobang, Zhao Ziyang, and so many others envisioned. As a result, its economy has grown at a record-breaking rate.

China's standing in the world community has recovered somewhat. However, the CPC is still viewed by many other governments with reserve and suspicion. The

CHINA'S ECONOMY IS LARGER THAN THAT OF

United States and many European nations still refuse to sell military equipment to China. However, the economic relationship between the United States and China has improved as China's needs have grown and the CPC has been more or less forced into observing more capitalistic principles. Nevertheless, the United States maintains its position that the CPC's cold-blooded handling of the Tiananmen demonstrations and refusal to take any responsibility for the massacre are unacceptable.

Every society must have its laws and regulations. But when people are under constant threat of beatings, torture, or even death at the hands of the very officials who are supposed to be serving them, they are no longer truly living at all. This was the fear that those who perished at Tiananmen Square were fighting against. Many of those who survived continue to battle it today. All they want is what millions around the world already have—the right to think, to speak, and to act without fear of punishment.

To some, Tiananmen Square will always be a reminder of the horrible events of 1989.

中华人民共和国万岁　　毛　　世界人民大团结万岁

INFLUENTIAL INDIVIDUALS

Hu Yaobang

Mao Zedong (1893–1976) was the leader of the Communist Party of China until his death. He was the primary founder of the People's Republic of China and the author of a collection of political beliefs known as Maoism.

Deng Xiaoping (1904–1997) was one of the leading figures in the Communist Party of China from the 1970s until the early 1990s. He championed reform of China's economy, moving it from the limitations of Maoism into a more opportunistic, free market type of system.

Hu Yaobang (1915–1989) was one of the most influential figures in the Communist Party of China who favored reform. He was forced to resign his position in the CPC in 1987 after refusing an order from Deng Xiaoping to punish three intellectuals who were openly critical of the Chinese government. His death sparked public demonstrations that led directly to the Tiananmen Square massacre.

Zhao Ziyang (1919–2005) was one of the highest-ranking members of the CPC during the 1980s and one of the most reliable supporters of Deng Xiaoping's economic reforms. However, he lost political power during the Tiananmen situation when he refused to implement martial law and instead went to Tiananmen Square to speak with the demonstrators.

Zhao Ziyang

Mikhail Gorbachev (1931–) was the leader of the Communist Party of the Soviet Union from 1985 until 1991. Although a communist all his life, he played a major role in disposing of communism as the Soviet system of government and in leading Russia into a more market-oriented economy. He won the Nobel Peace Prize in 1990 for his efforts.

Fang Lizhi (1936–2012) was a professor of astrophysics who wrote numerous essays and gave many speeches critical of the CPC while urging citizens to support the transition to a more democratic society.

Mikhail Gorbachev

TIMELINE

1976
Mao Zedong dies.

1977
Deng Xiaoping takes power.

1978
Deng implements the first stage of his economic reforms.

1989

April 15 Hu Yaobang dies following a heart attack.

April 17 Thousands gather in Tiananmen to mourn Hu's death and celebrate his legacy.

April 22 The CPC gives Hu a formal state funeral.

April 26 The CPC issues an editorial condemning the demonstrators and accusing them of trying to topple the current government.

May 13 Students begin a hunger strike in an attempt to regain national attention and support.

May 15 The CPC is forced to change the location of a welcoming ceremony for Soviet leader Mikhail Gorbachev due to the ongoing demonstrations in Tiananmen Square.

May 17 CPC leaders gather to discuss how best to handle the Tiananmen situation and decide to declare a state of martial law.

May 19 Zhao Ziyang makes a personal visit to ask demonstrators one last time to leave the square, but he is unsuccessful.

May 20 Military forces move through the streets of Beijing toward Tiananmen Square but are blocked by supporters of the demonstrators.

1984

Deng implements the second stage of his economic reforms.

1985-1986

First public demonstration by Chinese students in favor of democracy.

1989 continued

June 1 CPC leaders decide to use greater force to end the Tiananmen demonstrations.

June 3 Military forces again move through Beijing toward Tiananmen Square; when they encounter more resistance, they open fire, killing hundreds of people.

June 4 Military forces reach Tiananmen Square and violence continues in and around the area; by daybreak, most of the demonstrators have been cleared out; as word spreads of the attacks, the CPC is severely criticized by the governments of most other leading nations.

1989-1990

The CPC undertakes a campaign to cleanse the party of all people who were sympathetic to the demonstrators; they also roll back many of the personal freedoms that had been permitted during the reform period, as well as some of the economic improvements that had been made.

LIVING HISTORY

Primary sources provide firsthand evidence about a topic. Witnesses to a historical event create primary sources. They include autobiographies, newspaper reports of the time, oral histories, photographs, and memoirs. A secondary source analyzes primary sources, and is one step or more removed from the event. Secondary sources include textbooks, encyclopedias, and commentaries. To view the following primary and secondary sources, go to www.factsfornow.scholastic.com. Enter the keywords **Tiananmen Square Massacre** and look for the Living History logo Σ.

Σ **The April 26 Editorial** The April 26 editorial was supposed to scare the Tiananmen Square demonstrators. Instead, it only served to make them angrier. You can read an English translation of the editorial online.

Σ **Deng Xiaoping's Four Basic Principles** After taking over the Chinese government, Deng Xiaoping began a series of reforms. In a 1979 speech, he outlined his view of the CPC's role in governing the country and his future goals for leadership. You can read an English translation of part of the speech online.

Σ **Eyewitness Reports** Some foreign reporters were in China during the Tiananmen Square massacre to cover the arrival of Mikhail Gorbachev. They wrote about the massacre as it developed, providing a firsthand look at the violence. You can read one reporter's account online.

Σ **Fang Lizhi's "Democracy, Reform, and Modernization"** Fang Lizhi's writings and speeches inspired many early pro-democracy protesters. A 1986 speech at Tongji University in Shanghai became one of his most famous works. You can read an English translation of the speech online.

RESOURCES

Books

Berlatsky, Noah, ed. *China*. Detroit: Greenhaven Press, 2010.

Grant, R. G. *Communism*. Milwaukee, WI: World Almanac Library, 2006.

Hay, Jeff. *The Tiananmen Square Protests of 1989*. Detroit: Greenhaven Press, 2010.

Mara, Wil. *People's Republic of China.* New York: Children's Press, 2012.

Visit this Scholastic Web site for more information on the Tiananmen Square massacre:
www.factsfornow.scholastic.com
Enter the keywords **Tiananmen Square Massacre**

GLOSSARY

capitalism (KAP-i-tuh-liz-uhm) a way of organizing a country's economy so that most of the land, houses, factories, and other property belong to individuals and private companies rather than to the government

communist (KAHM-yuh-nist) relating to a way of organizing the economy of a country so that all land, property, businesses, and resources belong to the government or community, and the profits are shared by all

democracy (di-MAH-kruh-see) a form of government in which people choose their leaders in elections

demonstrations (dem-uhn-STRAY-shuhnz) gatherings in which people join together to protest something

economy (i-KAHN-uh-mee) the system of buying, selling, making things, and managing money in a place

editorial (ed-i-TOR-ee-uhl) an article that gives the opinion of the writer or of a newspaper, rather than just reporting facts in the news

free market (FREE MAHR-kit) an economic system characterized by pricing based on supply and demand rather than prices set by the government

hunger strike (HUNG-ger STRIKE) a situation in which a group of people refuse to eat in order to gain attention for a cause

inflation (in-FLAY-shuhn) a general increase in prices, causing money to be worth less

investment (in-VEST-muhnt) the giving or lending of money to something, such as a company, with the intention of getting more money back later

reform (re-FORM) improvement, or the correcting of something unsatisfactory

INDEX

Page numbers in *italics* indicate illustrations.

ABOUT THE AUTHOR

Wil Mara has written more than 140 books, many of which are educational titles for young readers. He is the author of the best-selling novel *Wave*, which won the New Jersey Notable Book Award, as well as the critically acclaimed thriller *The Gemini Virus*. He has also ghostwritten five of the popular Boxcar Children Mysteries. He has had a lifelong interest in Asian history and also wrote the book on China for Scholastic's Enchantment of the World series.